FORENSIC EVIDENCE
PRINTS

JOHN TOWNSEND

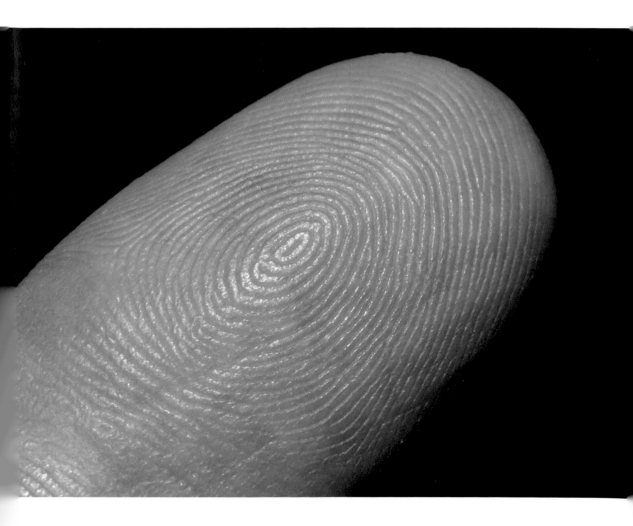

🌳 Crabtree Publishing Company

www.crabtreebooks.com

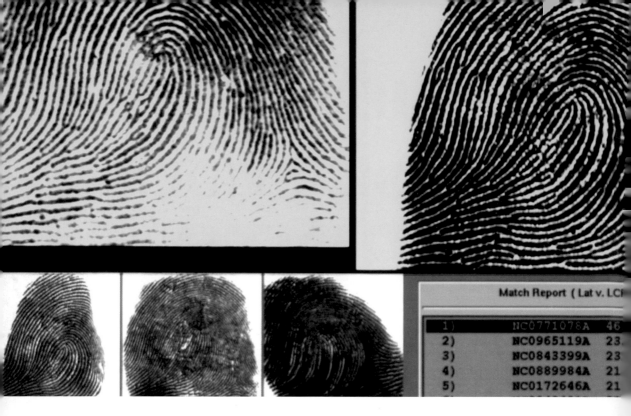

Match Report (Lat v. LCI

1)	NC0771078A	46
2)	NC0965119A	23
3)	NC0843399A	23
4)	NC0889984A	21
5)	NC0172646A	21

Crabtree Publishing Company
PMB 16A,
350 Fifth Avenue,
Suite 3308
New York, NY 10118

616 Welland Avenue,
St. Catharines, Ontario
L2M 5V6

Content development by
Shakespeare Squared

www.ShakespeareSquared.com

Published by Crabtree
Publishing Company © 2008

First published in Great Britain
in 2008 by ticktock Media Ltd,
2 Orchard Business Centre,
North Farm Road,
Tunbridge Wells, Kent, TN2 3XF

ticktock project editor:
    Ruth Owen
ticktock project designer:
    Sara Greasley
ticktock picture researcher:
    Lizzie Knowles

With thanks to: Series Editors Honor Head and J
ean Coppendale and Consultant John Cassella,
Principal Lecturer in Forensic Science, Department
of Forensic Science, Staffordshire University, UK

Picture credits (t=top; b=bottom; c=centre; l=left; r=right):
Michael Donne / Science Photo Library: 7, 22b. Martin Dohrn
/ Science Photo Library: 8-9. Mauro Fermariello / Science Photo
Library: 12, 13. David R. Frazier / Science Photo Library: 25t.
Mitsuaki Iwago / Minden Pictures / FLPA: 11br. James King-
Holmes / Science Photo Library: 15 main, 16, 18-19 main.
Pasieka / Science Photo Library: OFC. Philippe Psaila / Science
Photo Library: 17b, 21t, 21b. Paul Rapson / Science Photo
Library: 6. Shutterstock: 1, 2, 4-5 all, 10 all, 11t, 11cr, 11bl, 14,
15t, 17t, 19t, 20 all, 22t, 23t, 23b, 25b, 27, 28 all, 29 all, 31 all.
Upper Cut Images/ Getty Images: 24. Jim Varney / Science
Photo Library: 26.

Every effort has been made to trace copyright holders, and we
apologize in advance for any omissions. We would be pleased
to insert the appropriate acknowledgments in any subsequent
edition of this publication.

Library and Archives Canada Cataloguing in Publication
Townsend, John, 1955-
    Forensic evidence : prints / John Townsend.

(Crabtree contact)
Includes index.
ISBN 978-0-7787-3811-4 (bound).
--ISBN 978-0-7787-3833-6 (pbk.)

    1. Criminal investigation--Juvenile literature. 2. Footprints--
Identification--Juvenile literature. 3. Fingerprints--Identification--
Juvenile literature. 4. Forensic sciences--Juvenile literature. I. Title.
II. Series.

HV8073.8.T693 2008   j363.25'8   C2008-901217-8

Library of Congress Cataloging-in-Publication Data

Townsend, John, 1955-
  Forensic evidence : prints / John Townsend.
      p. cm. -- (Crabtree contact)
  Includes index.
  ISBN-13: 978-0-7787-3833-6 (pbk. : alk. paper)
  ISBN-10: 0-7787-3833-7 (pbk. : alk. paper)
  ISBN-13: 978-0-7787-3811-4 (reinforced library binding : alk. paper)
  ISBN-10: 0-7787-3811-6 (reinforced library binding : alk. paper)
  1. Criminal investigation--Juvenile literature. 2. Footprints--
Identification--Juvenile literature. 3. Fingerprints--Identification--Juvenile
literature. 4. Forensic sciences--Juvenile literature. I. Title. II. Series.

HV8073.8.T684 2008
363.25'8--dc22

                                        2008006297

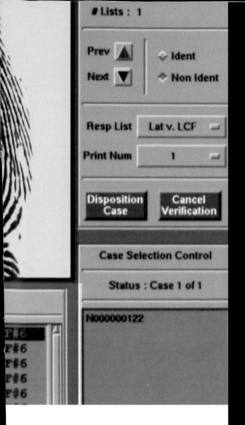

Contents

CHAPTER 1

ROBBERY!

"Everybody down on the floor. NOW!"

A robber wearing a mask bursts into a bank.

He is carrying a gun. He points the gun to make everyone lie on the floor. He forces the bank workers to put the money into bags.

The police speed to the bank.

The robber gets away with thousands of dollars!

He speeds away from the crime scene in a getaway car. A second masked robber drives the car.

The police find the getaway car just outside the city. It has been set on fire. The police think the robbers set fire to the car...

...to destroy all the evidence!

CHAPTER 2

FINGERPRINTS

The car the robbers used was stolen! The stolen car is now a **crime scene**.

Crime Scene Investigators (CSIs) get to work on the car. They are looking for **forensic evidence** such as fingerprints.

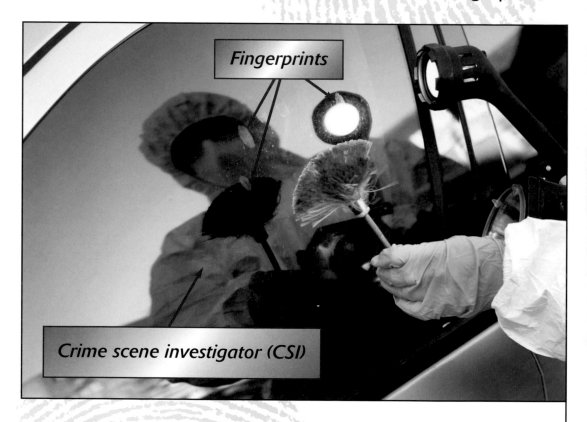

Fingerprints

Crime scene investigator (CSI)

One CSI brushes **fingerprint powder** onto one of the car's windows. He uses a special lamp to make fingerprints show up.

Did the robbers touch the car with their bare hands? If they did, their sweaty fingers will have left fingerprints behind.

A fingerprint is lifted from one of the car's seatbelts. The CSI uses sticky tape to lift the print.

Sticky tape

The tape will be stuck to a piece of card called a **lift card**.

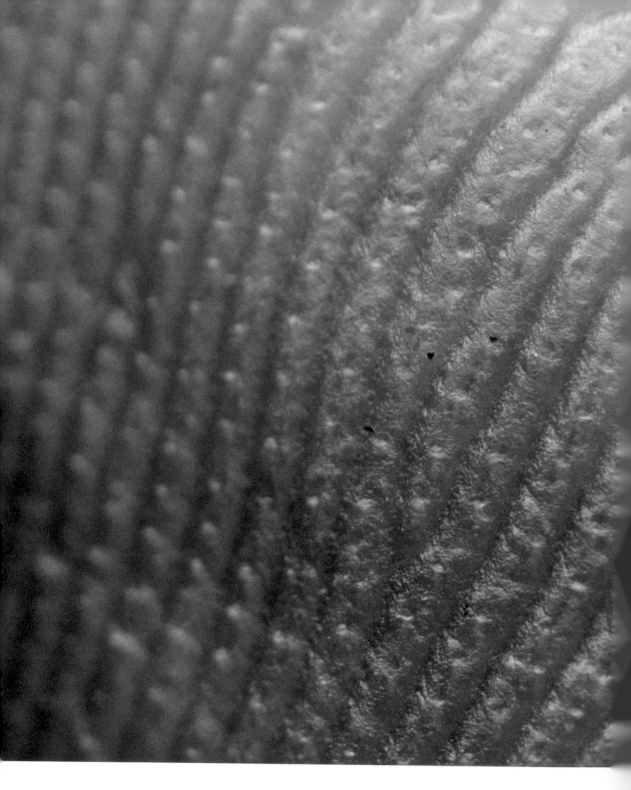

Our fingerprint patterns are made by skin ridges.
The sweat comes from **sweat glands**.
No two people have the same fingerprint pattern.
Even **identical twins** have different fingerprints.

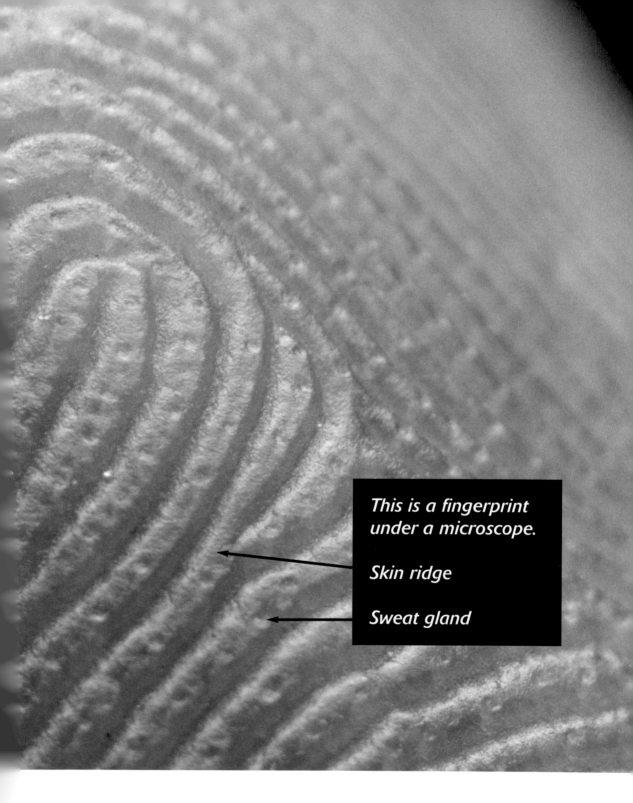

This is a fingerprint under a microscope.

Skin ridge

Sweat gland

Our fingerprints form before we are born.
They stay the same our entire lives.
They only change if our fingers are
burnt or scarred.

There are three main fingerprint patterns.

Arches

This pattern has ridges which enter from one side of the print and go off the other side. The ridges make an arch shape.

Loops

This pattern has a ridge that starts on one side. It makes a loop then goes back off on the same side.

Whorls

This pattern has ridges that make a complete circle.

Fingerprints have a main pattern and a lot of other tiny details.

Dot

Bifurcation

Short ridge

Bridge

Ridge ending

IS THAT A FACT?

Koala fingerprints are just like human prints. Even with a microscope, it's difficult to tell them apart!

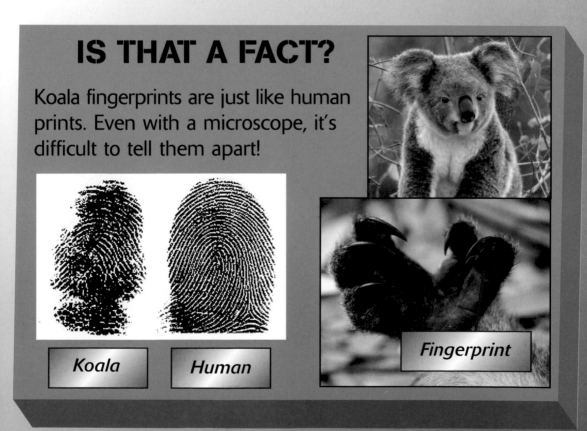

Koala

Human

Fingerprint

CHAPTER 3

AT THE CRIME LAB

The fingerprints found on the car are taken to the **crime lab**.

First, the fingerprints will be compared with fingerprints from the car owner and his family.

The fingerprints are scanned and put into a computer program.

Fingerprint analyst

A **fingerprint analyst** compares the fingerprint from the seatbelt with one from the car owner. **It's a skillful job.**

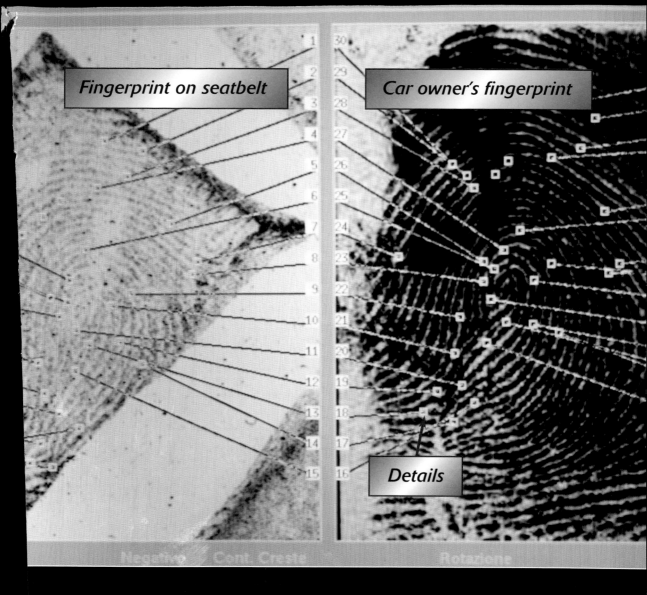

Fingerprint on seatbelt

Car owner's fingerprint

Details

The details on the two prints are carefully compared.

They are a match!

RESULT
The fingerprint on the seatbelt wasn't from the robbers. It belongs to the car owner. All the fingerprints on the car are from the owner or his family.

The police find a leather glove near the getaway car.

Could this be a breakthrough?

They check the security video from the bank. The glove is just like one worn by the robber. The robber thought he was clever wearing gloves, but guess what the police find on the glove…

…fingerprints!

The prints can be compared to fingerprints on a **police database**. This database contains the fingerprints of thousands of **known criminals**.

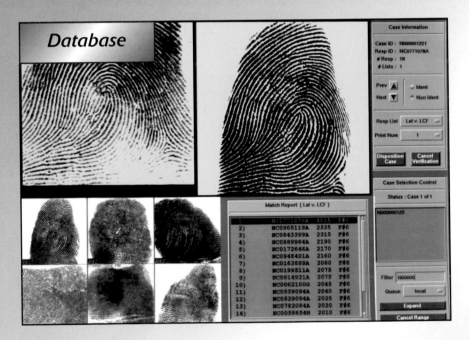

If the bank robbers have committed a crime in the past, their fingerprints will be on the database.

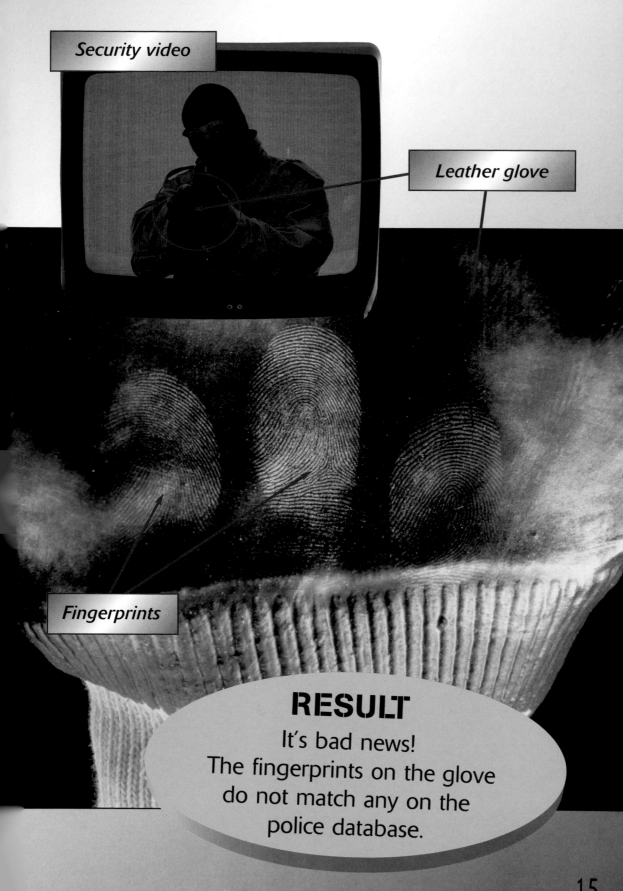

Another way to test for prints is using **magnetic** powder.

This works on difficult surfaces such as plastic bags, magazines, and even waxy fruit.

Tiny iron flakes stick to the print. Then the soft, magnetic brush picks up all the loose flakes. The print made of iron flakes is left behind.

Magnetic brush

Unlike old-fashioned dusting brushes, this brush doesn't touch or harm the print.

Print of iron flakes

The CSIs find a CD in the car. The CD does not belong to the car's owner.

There are fingerprints on the CD.

Crime reconstruction

The fingerprints on the CD don't belong to the car owner or his family. They don't match any prints on the police database. They don't match the prints on the glove. But they do match prints on the car's **false number plate**.

RESULT
The police think they may have the prints of the second robber who drove the getaway car.

The crime scene investigators keep searching.

Near the car they find **a banana** under a bush.
It's a funny place to find a banana!

Using magnetic powder, they dust the banana skin.
Three fingerprints show up!

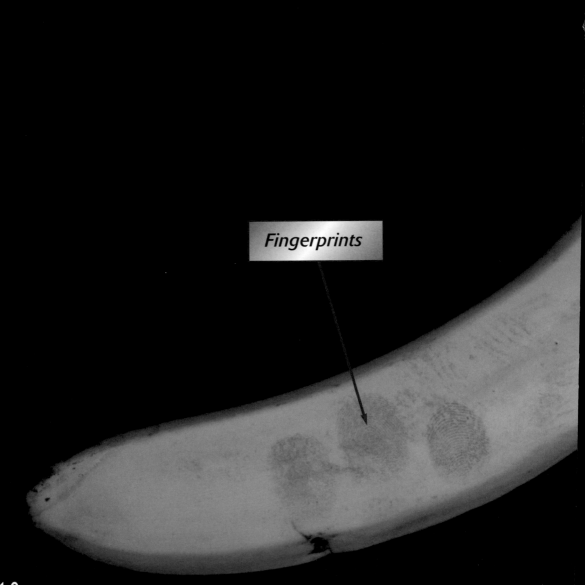

Fingerprints

Did one of the robbers decide he didn't have time for a snack?

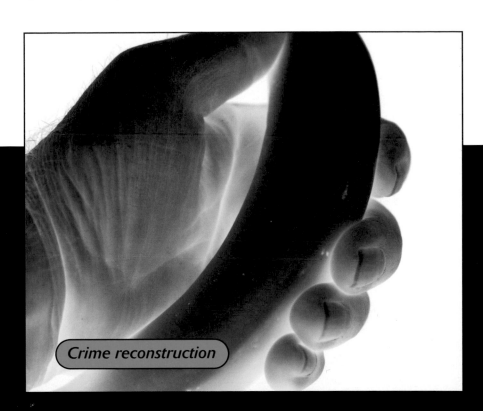

Crime reconstruction

RESULT
The prints on the banana match the prints on the gloves!

Close to where the CSIs find the banana, they find torn envelopes.

Some of the stolen money was in envelopes. Fingerprints don't show up on paper. But a chemical called DFO reacts with sweat from fingers.

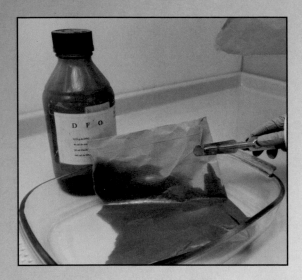

At the lab, the torn envelopes are dipped in DFO. Then an **ultraviolet light** is shone on the paper.

Fingerprints on paper glow orange under ultraviolet light.

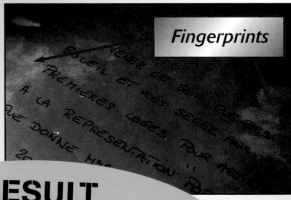

Fingerprints

RESULT
Both robbers' prints are on the torn envelopes. The robbers couldn't wait to count their money!

Crime reconstruction —
the robbers tore
open the envelopes
to count the money!

The CSIs make another discovery.

Just where the getaway car had been waiting, the police find a soda can.

It has the driver's **fingerprints all over it!**

Crime reconstruction

The can is photographed with measurements.
The photos record the position and size of the prints.

It's not just the driver's fingerprints on the can.
His **lip prints** are there, too.

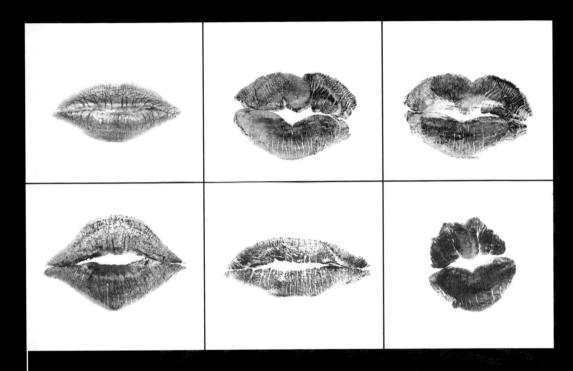

Our lip prints are unique just like our fingerprints.

IS THAT A FACT?

Police have caught criminals from prints of their toes, knees, ears, and tongues!

CHAPTER 4

AN ARREST!

The police have prints from the two robbers.
But they have no idea who the men are.

Then there is a breakthrough!

The police stop a man for driving too fast.
He tries to run off. The police catch and **arrest him.**

An officer takes his prints with a fingerprinting machine. It sends the prints straight to the police database.

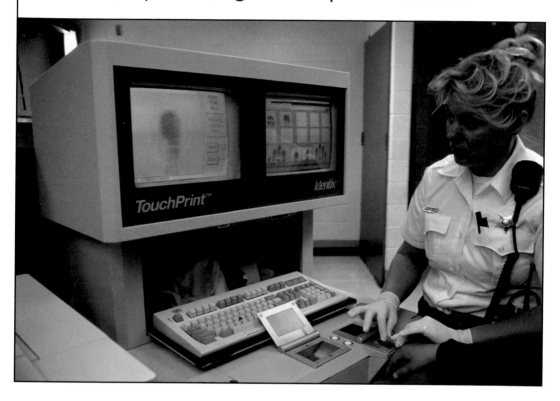

The computer sends a message.

The man's prints match one of the bank robber's!

The man's cell phone leads the police to his friend. His friend's prints match the other robber's prints.

RESULT
The police now have two suspects!

CHAPTER 5

SHOEPRINTS

Both men say they are not the bank robbers.

The first man arrested shouts,
"You can't prove I was near that bank."

But the police can!

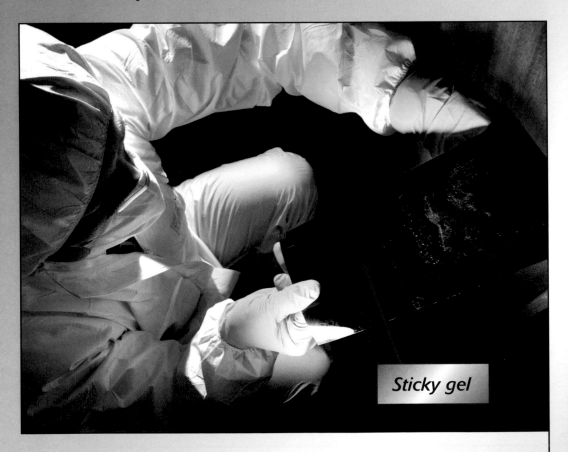

Sticky gel

The robber left a muddy shoeprint on the floor of the bank.
One of the CSIs collected the shoeprint as evidence.
He used special paper covered in sticky gel to lift the print.

Just like our fingerprints, our shoeprints are unique, too.

As we walk around, our shoes get damaged by stones or bits of glass.

This damage is unique to our shoes.

RESULT

The shoeprint is matched to the suspect's shoe. It proves the suspect was in the bank.

CHAPTER 6

ON TRIAL

In court, the two men are found guilty of the robbery.

Evidence: Suspect A – The Robber	MATCH
Fingerprints on glove by getaway car	✓
Fingerprints on banana by getaway car	✓
Fingerprints on envelopes by getaway car	✓
Shoeprint in the bank	✓

Verdict: PRINTS PROVE GUILT
(Money from the bank robbery is found buried in his garden.)

Evidence: Suspect B – Getaway driver	MATCH
Fingerprints on CD in getaway car	✓
Fingerprints on false number plate of getaway car	✓
Fingerprints on envelopes by getaway car	✓
Fingerprints and lip prints on drink can outside bank	✓

Verdict: PRINTS PROVE GUILT

CASE SOLVED!

NEED-TO-KNOW WORDS

crime lab A laboratory with equipment that is used for scientific experiments and tests on crime scene evidence.

crime scene Any place where a crime has happened. This could be a room, a car, or a big area such as a field.

crime scene investigators (CSIs) People who examine crime scenes and collect evidence

evidence Facts and signs that can show what happened during a crime

false number plate a made-up registration number on a car. This false number cannot be traced by the police.

fingerprint analyst An expert at matching fingerprints

fingerprint powder A fine dust that sticks to fingerprints. It is used to show fingerprints more clearly.

forensic evidence Detailed facts and signs that can show what happened in a crime

guilty Having done wrong, such as committing a crime

known criminal A person who has been convicted of a crime in the past. The person's details, such as fingerprints, are kept on a police database.

lift card A card on which a fingerprint is stored once it has been "lifted" from a crime scene

magnetic Something that attracts iron or steel

suspect A person who is thought to have carried out a crime

sweat gland A part of the skin that gives off sweat through a tiny hole called a pore

ultraviolet light A special light which shines deep purple, making some objects glow in the dark. It is sometimes called a black light.

unique The only one of its kind

verdict The final decision of what happened

NEED-TO-KNOW PRINT FACTS

- **Visible fingerprints**
  Sometimes fingerprints are patent — you can see them. They can be made in blood or left in a soft surface, such as a piece of chewing gum or a bar of chocolate.

- **Unseen fingerprints**
  Fingerprints that cannot be seen are called latent prints. CSIs use special dusting powder or chemicals that turn the print a color that can be seen.

- **Shoe databases**
  When you buy a pair of shoes it has a sole pattern. The makers of the shoes store these patterns on databases. Investigators can use the database to match a shoeprint with a sole pattern. This will tell them the make of a shoe.

- **Tire marks**
  Car tires make prints in mud and sand. The pattern of the tread can prove what make of tire made the print. Cuts, holes, and worn parts of the tire will show up, too. This will make each tire print unique.

PRINTS ONLINE

http://www.cyberbee.com/whodunnit/fp.html
All you need to know about fingerprints

http://www.fbi.gov/kids/6th12th/6th12th.htm
How the FBI investigates crimes

http://www.howstuffworks.com/csi5.htm
All about the world of CSI

http://www.crimelibrary.com/criminal_mind/forensics/crimescene/6.html
All about crime scene analysis

INDEX

Printed in the U.S.A.